The Pond at Cape May Point

The Pond at Cape May Point

Fred Caruso, paintings

Burt Kimmelman, poems

Marsh Hawk Press • New York • 2002

02 03 04 7 6 5 4 3 2 1

Marsh Hawk Press books are published by Poetry Mailing List, Inc.,
a not-for-profit corporation under United States Internal Revenue Code.

Text set in Garamond
Book design: Sandy McIntosh

Authors photograph: John F. Morariu, Jr.
Printed in the United States by McNaughton & Gunn
Grateful acknowledgement is made to the following publications where
some of these poems and paintings have appeared: the *Newark Review*,
poetrynow and *Sugar Mule*.

Library of Congress Cataloging-in-Publication Data
Kimmelman, Burt.
The pond at Cape May Point / Fred Caruso, paintings ; Burt Kimmelman,
poems.
p. cm.
ISBN 0-9713332-4-6
1. Cape May Point (N.J.)—Poetry. 2. Nature—Poetry. 3.
Ponds—Poetry. I. Caruso, Fred. II. Title.
PS3561.I4233 P66 2002
811'.54—dc21

2002002676

Marsh Hawk Press
P.O. Box 220, Stuyvesant Station
New York, NY 10009
www.marshhawkpress.org

❧

Morning at the Pond

At the edge they poke
their beaks down

to pond bottom, its

muddy cache
of tendrils and worms,

then raise up

their heads to eat, look
around—drops

of water falling

back to the
sun's bright surfaces.

Pine Tree

From the ground
of fallen
pine needles
a leap up

flapping wings
to the tree's
lowest branch
hidden there.

Rain

The splashes and circles
in the water

among the shoots of grass
by the shoreline

signaling where to look—
a loose feather

floating among the swirls—
the tern places

first one leg, the other,
making her way.

Geese

The geese move steadily overhead,
their raucous signaling cutting short
the pond's quiet routine, and descend

together all at once, breaking the

water's plane in small splashes across
the wide curve of their crescent, float, look
around, and suddenly become still.

Afternoon Haze

Sky a single color—
and below, the trees thick

across water and sun—

shoots of bramble springing
up against the mud shore.

Feeding

Beak under
water, the

swan wags its

head back and

forth, tearing

the hidden
roots below.

Swirl of Water

Feathers up
in a fan,
the swan swims

after geese,
ducks—ousting
all creatures

from the swirl
of water
around her.

Dawn

The island—its rock
and bush, grass and moss—
in water's mirror

where algae and twigs,
weeds and mist, somehow
have drifted away.

Morning Pond

Circles in
the still shine—
wings overhead.

The Wind

Across the pond the tree
surges and twists as if

the sea, in agony,

or some other unkempt
creature, has come to stay.

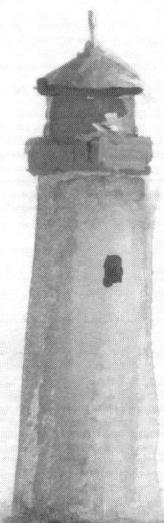

Something

The slate rock takes in sunlight
in an endless darkness but
for a white cut line across
its base. Something will grow there.

After the Storm

Rain gone, the white flowers
on the brambles bow forward
over a mallard floating by
beside its image in the water.

Sudden Noise

Floating on the shadows of trees,
the far below current running
to the pond's deep center, the swan
turns his head toward the bank of sun
and sand—a sound already gone—
where, in a thicket of bramble
and blossom, some ducks are resting.

Hunting

Wings open
against
all winds,
the egret

rises up
over
its prey
then tumbles

far below
the bright
surface
of water.

Bath

Beneath the branch—whose leaves turn
the light askance among moss
and grass—the duck's bill searches
within the roughed-up feathers,
tugging at the wet and warm.

Scrub Pine

The humming
bird rises
slowly to
the branch of
pine needles.

The sparrow
hovers at
the pine tree's
topmost branch
then flies on.

Trees are wings
as they bow
to the sea's
salted wind,
standing there.

Early Morning at the Pond

Stuttering cheeps
All wings flapping
Heading away.

Intruders

The pigeons have landed on the island,
come down from the treetops
jutting into the sky
covering the far edges of the pond,

to settle for awhile along the skirt
of mud—grass, moss and rock
pacing the shore's image
in water—ducks, geese and swans gliding by.

Wounded Bird

Water covers
what it can
and makes the shore
where the bird,

wounded, standing
on its one
good leg, each day

finds within
the mud the life
of insects
to its liking.

Whatever

Torrents below,
untouched by light
or wind riffling
the pond's surface
and bending flight—

goose and swan, tern
and sparrow, test
the skirt of mud
for whatever
has lost its way.

Daylight

Above the treetops
the ducks descend
to the mirror plane

of daylight branching
within the shadows
keeping to the shore.

Egret

From seaward before the storm—
wings outspread over water
in slow, muscular movement—

the egret closes in on

the pond's far shore, touches down,
stands tall, enfolding itself,
its white oval silhouette.

Morning Light

Crocus
winding over
and over—

morning
light slides along
the current—

sleeping
birds under trees
on the shore.

Squall

Wind cutting
across water—
ducks turn their

backs, huddling
under pines
leaning in—

a gull floats
along, then
lifts itself

toward the sea,
leaving dark
deep behind.